ENDORSEMENTS

Pastor Mackenzie Kambizi has written this book to eliminate the paradox that many Christians face; living a Christian life that does not announce the gospel. While many people desire to share their faith with others, they lack the appropriate knowledge and skills to enable them do so effectively and efficiently. This deficiency has led to general apathy towards witnessing, which is the essence of any committed Christian. This book has been developed to meet this gap and is solely dedicated to assisting Christians fulfill the command of the Lord to find people. The book is replete with timely nuggets on personal evangelism and seeks to empower every Christian to be an effective soul winner. Pastor Kambizi has designed relevant and practical Bible studies in order to equip present-day Christians for a post-modern target audience. He has tapped into his perceptive knowledge of the scriptures and brought his rich cross-cultural ministry to the fore. His vantage point as a modern preacher and a renowned world evangelist, has enabled him to develop Bible-based principles that will benefit Christians who seek to engage in a lifestyle of evangeliving. The greatest evidence of a transformed life is the ability to tell others about the transforming power of God. It is without doubt that this resource manual stands at the cutting edge of appropriate Christian material that will benefit those who are willing to be used as the feet of Jesus in bringing hope to others in a gracious and poignant manner.

— *Isaac Chiyokoma*
Chaplain, Rusangu University

"People write books either out of desire to share their untested thoughts which they are certain about or to share thoughts and methods that have worked for them over and over again. Mackenzie Kambizi is a successful evangelist of many years across the globe. He evangelizes regularly all over the continents. I have seen him in action and I have been infected by his passion. What he has written in this book are methods that have been tested, improved and proven to effectively work in many parts of the world. When biblical concepts meet a practical approach as done in this book, then what remains is for the reader to apply. This book is many years experience, conveniently delivered to us!"

— **Rei Kesis,**
PhD., Baraton University Chaplain

Mackenzie Kambizi tackles a subject that is near and dear to his heart. "Push the kingdom" has been his mantra and practice in ministry. He has engaged in evangelism in different parts of the world under different contexts and cultures and draws from this vast experience and from scripture practical principles for personal evangelism. This book will equip and inspire you to action. It will challenge you to move out of your comfort zone.

— **Farai Nhiwatiwa, Senior Pastor,**
Grand Rapids Bethel SDA Church

Pastor Kambizi
My father is a patient, compassionate and kind father. He has such a wild and complete zest for life it's unreal. My daddy has taught me so much and i have even more left to learn, from him. I love his preaching and teaching. This book will be the same - great tool. I love you, my daddy

— **Morgan Mutsa Kambizi,**
Daughter

FOUND
PEOPLE
FIND
PEOPLE

FOUND PEOPLE ~ FIND PEOPLE

Intentional <u>PERSONAL</u> Evangelism

14 Meetings
PRAYER AND BIBLE STUDY
Practical! Relevant! Biblical!

#PushTheKingdom
Mackenzie Kambizi

EQUIP PRESS

Colorado Springs

FOUND PEOPLE ~ FIND PEOPLE

Copyright © 2019 and Mackenzie Kambizi

All rights reserved. No part of this publication may be reproduced, distributed, or transmitted in any form or by any means, without prior written permission.

Published by Equip Press, Colorado Springs, CO

Scripture quotations marked (ESV) are taken from The ESV® Bible (The Holy Bible, English Standard Version®) copyright © 2001 by Crossway, a publishing minis-try of Good News Publishers. ESV® Text Edition: 2011. The ESV® text has been reproduced in cooperation with and by permission of Good News Publishers.
Unauthorized reproduction of this publication is prohibited. Used by permission.
All rights reserved.

Scripture quotations marked (KJV) are taken from the King James Bible. Accessed on Bible Gateway at www.BibleGateway.com.

Scripture quotations marked (NASB) are taken from the New American Standard Bible® (NASB), copyright © 1960, 1962, 1963, 1968, 1971, 1972, 1973, 1975, 1977, 1995 by The Lockman Foundation, www.Lockman.org. Used by permission.

Scripture quotations marked (NIV) are taken from the Holy Bible, New International Version. Copyright © 1973, 1978, 1984, 2011 by Biblica, Inc.® Used by permission.
All rights reserved worldwide.

Scripture quotations marked (NKJV) are taken from the New King James Version®. Copyright © 1982 by Thomas Nelson, Inc. Used by permission. All rights reserved.

Scripture quotations marked (NLT) are taken from the Holy Bible, New Living Translation, copyright © 1996, 2004, 2015 by Tyndale House Foundation. Used by permission of Tyndale House Publishers, Inc., Carol Stream, Illinois 60188. All rights reserved.

Scripture quotations marked (NRSV) are taken from the New Revised Standard Version Bible, copyright © 1989 the Division of Christian Education of the National Council of the Churches of Christ in the United States of America. Used by permission. All rights reserved.

First Edition: 2019
Found People Find People / Mackenzie Kambizi
Paperback ISBN: 978-1-946453-65-5
eBook ISBN: 978-1-946453-66-2

DEDICATION

I dedicate this manual to God. His love for me and His salvation made me an evangelist by His grace. My deep appreciation also goes to every witness of God who desires to make Him known through their personal witnessing. May you influence one person at a time until all the ransomed ones of God be saved to sin no more, and faith becomes sight, hope becomes reality, and love conquers all!

Push the Kingdom! God loves every person like crazy!

Matthew 10:32

Confess Christ Before Men

32 "Therefore whoever confesses Me before men, him I will also confess before My Father who is in heaven. 33 But whoever denies Me before men, him I will also deny before My Father who is in heaven.

It's true the only thing we won't do in heaven is EVANGELISM—let's do it whilst we still have time!

14 MEETINGS
PRAYER AND BIBLE FEASTING

SMALL GROUP DAILY PROGRAM

	ACTIVITY	TIME
1.	**Welcome of the Audience**	2 minutes
2.	**Opening Song**	3 minutes
3.	**Intercessory Prayer Ministry**	10 minutes
	• Introduce the intercessory prayer theme of the day.	
	• Read and explain briefly the Bible promise or text that goes together with the prayer theme.	
	• Ask each person to write on the prepared prayer request paper just the **initial** (e.g. **P** for Peter) of the people they wish to be presented before the Lord during intercessory prayer. Please avoid writing full names for confidentiality purposes. Ask everyone present to write. Every participant is also free to include their initials where it suits them.	
	• Put the papers in a box or bowl and mix the papers together well.	

ACTIVITY	TIME
• Request the audience to form prayer partners and pray for two of the papers they choose. No one should belong to the same pair daily. You are free to keep changing the format of prayer groups for variety's sake.	
• After the prayer session, collect all the papers and put them back into a prayer requests box for a special prayer session at church. Destroy the papers after the church service.	
• Request people to return to their seats.	
4. **Read John 14:26 and 16:13 daily:** • Ask each person to pray that God provides them with the right learning attitude, and for the guidance of the Holy Spirit during the duration of the discussion.	2 minutes
5. **Do a bit of housekeeping before the study begins:**	3 minutes
• Ensure that each person has a study guide or sits close to one.	
• Ensure that all the people have Bibles or are seated close to one.	
• Let the audience know that they are free to submit written questions to be answered the following day. Supply prepared papers to everyone present.	

ACTIVITY	TIME
6. **Introduce and present the study:**	**40 minutes**
• Use the lecture format since the content is fairly new to others.	
• Involve the audience in reading the Bible and certain sections of the study guide.	
• Keep checking to see that your audience understands the language and the concepts. Ask review questions.	
• If the audience is manageable, allow them to ask questions of clarity, which are meant to help them to understand.	
• Questions that challenge or refute your content should be written down so that you have enough time to provide a well-researched response. Avoid being put into an argumentative mode, but appreciate people for asking.	
• Do not read every line and text on the study guide. Concentrate on key statements and texts. The participants will read the whole presentation on their own.	
• However, avoid over-summarizing the content.	
7. **Review and application of the lesson:**	
• Take a moment to review the lesson. Let the participants fill in a prepared response paper, which is designed to guide the lesson review.	

ACTIVITY	TIME
• The review paper also has a space that asks the participants to write their personal commitment to the discoveries they have personally made during the study. Do not force anyone to make your preferred decision. Each one should discover from the lesson the kind of decision they should make.	
8. **Conduct a session of prayer to mark the end of the service:**	5 minutes
• Ask people to identify something to praise and thank God for.	
• Entertain some personal prayer requests that do not offend the people's confidentiality or dignity.	
• Ask a few people to share the joy of their discoveries in the lesson of the day.	
• Request two or three people to offer short prayers.	
• Announce the topic for the next day.	
9. **Where possible, serve refreshments to allow fellowship and bonding. Please mix and mingle, in order to get to know people better.**	25 minutes
10. **Remember, this is just a guide. Do what whatever works.**	

CONTENTS

1. Knowing Our Origins — 19
2. God's Reason for Creating Us — 23
3. What Really Went Wrong? — 27
4. A Friend You Can Trust Forever — 31
5. Avoiding Risky Behaviors — 35
6. Your Safest Guide to Life And Real Peace — 39
7. Enjoying Good Health — 43
8. Does The Sabbath Matter Any More? Part 1 — 47
9. Does The Sabbath Matter Any More? Part 2 — 55
10. Becoming A New Person — 63
11. The Pain Of Losing Loved Ones Through Death — 67
12. Understanding Our Times — 73
13. The Promise Of The Holy Spirit — 79
14. Free At Last — 85

FOUND PEOPLE FIND PEOPLE

FOREWORD/INTRODUCTION

I am greatly indebted to several persons who deepened my awareness of the gift of evangelism on my life. This witnessing manual/book idea resonated with my spirit after many evangelistic series throughout the world. After the demand of speaking invitations whilst pastoring full time became overwhelming to meet, I longed for a way of multiplying the impact and witness of the gospel. As I was reading the Book of John, the first chapter it all came together.

The First Disciples

35 Again, the next day, John stood with two of his disciples. 36 And looking at Jesus as He walked, he said, "Behold the Lamb of God!" 37 The two disciples heard him speak, and they followed Jesus. 38 Then Jesus turned, and seeing them following, said to them, "What do you seek?" They said to Him, "Rabbi" (which is translated, Teacher), "where are You staying?" 39 He said to them, "Come and see." They came and saw where He was staying, and remained with Him that day (now it was about the tenth hour). 40 One of the two who heard John speak, and followed Him, was Andrew, Simon Peter's brother. 41 *He first found his own brother Simon, and said to him, "We have found the [l] Messiah" (which is translated, the Christ).* 42 And he brought him to Jesus. Now when Jesus looked at him, He said, "You are Simon the son of Jonah. You shall be called Cephas" (which is translated, A Stone). 43 The following day Jesus wanted to go to Galilee, and *He found Philip and said to him, "Follow Me."* 44 Now Philip was from Bethsaida, the city of Andrew and Peter. 45 *Philip found Nathanael and said to him, "We have found Him of whom Moses in the law, and also the prophets, wrote—Jesus of Nazareth, the son of Joseph."*

46 And Nathanael said to him, "Can anything good come out of Nazareth?" ***Philip said to him, "Come and see."*** 47 Jesus saw Nathanael coming toward Him, and said of him, "Behold, an Israelite indeed, in whom is no deceit!" 48 Nathanael said to Him, "How do You know me?" Jesus answered and said to him, "Before Philip called you, when you were under the fig tree, I saw you." 49 Nathanael answered and said to Him, "Rabbi, You are the Son of God! You are the King of Israel!"

FOUND PEOPLE FIND PEOPLE! They went back to the people they knew, who were close to them and witnessed. Personal witnessing of Andrew brought Peter into a living relationship with Christ, and the personal witnessing of Phillip brought Nathaniel to the one he yearned for the most. Whose destiny is in your mouth? Whose purpose is tied up to your personal witnessing of Jesus Christ to them? We are saved to serve. Somebody somewhere is looking for what you've found, waiting for your personal introduction of the Savior Jesus Christ to them. Each one reach one! We can reach them in the gym, our homes, their homes, at work, on the bus, clubhouse, crack house, whorehouse, White House, church house, and anywhere people are found. The gospel still works!

Here are my five loaves and two fishes to offer them when you find them!

14 MEETINGS
PRAYER AND BIBLE FEASTING

MEETINGS PRAYER THEME SCHEDULE

Meeting	Prayer Theme	Bible Promise/Text
# 1	Pray for at least 3 people who are going through trying moments in their lives.	Isaiah 46:3-5
# 2	Pray for at least 3 people to make the right decisions that will make a positive change in their marriages, families, or in their single lives.	Deuteronomy 30:19-20
# 3	Pray for at least 3 people to resist the pressing temptations that are likely to ruin their lives.	1 Corinthians 10:13
# 4	Pray for at least 3 people to heal from the mistakes that have brought physical or emotional pain in their own lives, or in the lives of others.	Ezekiel 33:10-11
# 5	Pray for at least 3 people to overcome certain addictions in their lives.	Romans 7:18, 24-25a

# 6	Pray for at least 3 people to become Bible-believing Christians.	Psalm 119:105
# 7	Pray for at least 3 people to recover from health challenges.	3 John 2
# 8	Pray for at least 3 people to have rest and peace of mind.	Matthew 11:28-30; John 14:27
# 9	Pray for at least 3 people to develop good interpersonal skills so as to bring joy and happiness in their families.	Ephesians 4:29
# 10	Pray that God gives you humility to forgive people who have offended you. Or pray for the Holy Spirit to reconcile with the people you have offended.	Matthew 6:14-15; James 5:16
# 11	Pray for at least 3 people to heal from the loss of their loved ones through death or divorce.	1 Corinthians 10:13
# 12	Pray for at least 3 people who have been involved in some disaster or whose relatives have been affected by a disaster.	1 Timothy 2:1
# 13	Pray for at least 3 people to overcome an impossible situation in their lives. Pray for them to experience some miraculous breakthrough.	Genesis 18:13-14
# 14	Pray for at least 3 groups of people that you really want to see in heaven at the second coming of Christ.	Revelation 21:1-5

MEETING ONE

KNOWING OUR ORIGINS

1. **Who owns the universe?**
   - **Genesis 1:1–2, Psalm 19:1–2, and Romans 1:20**
     - ✓ The whole universe belongs to the Creator God who created it.
     - ✓ Nature reveals the glory and the knowledge of the Creator. Its design, systems, and natural laws could not have come by chance or by accident.
     - ✓ Even though the Creator God is invisible, nature is evidence of His existence.

2. **What makes the Creator God different from the other gods?**
   - **Genesis 1:1–2**
   He is the only God who is identified with the act of creation.
   - **Psalm 90:1–2**
   He is the only God who has no beginning and no end. He is coming from everlasting to everlasting. He was ever there before there was nature.
   - **1 Timothy 6:16**
   It is impossible for Him to die, even if He wanted to die. He is life itself.

3. **How did He create the universe and everything that is in it?**
   - **Psalm 33:6–9**
     - ✓ God the Creator spoke nature into existence.
     - ✓ This means that He created the visible and the invisible matter out of nothing.
     - ✓ His word has creative power. No one in the whole universe has such ability.

4. **What was the order of creation on Earth?**
   - **Genesis 1:1 – 2:1–3**
     The Creator took one literal week to form and create all things on the earth:
     - ✓ Day 1. Light
     - ✓ Day 2. Sky
     - ✓ Day 3. Seas, dry ground, and vegetation
     - ✓ Day 4. Sun, moon, and stars
     - ✓ Day 5. Birds and water creatures
     - ✓ Day 6. Land animals and people
     - ✓ Day 7. Sabbath – see also Exodus 20:11.

5. **How precious is human creation?**
   - **Genesis 1:26–28**
     - ✓ Human beings, both male and female, are the only creatures on earth that resemble God. We did not come from animals, as evolution would want us to believe.
     - ✓ The Creator appointed human beings in charge over all His created works on earth.
   - **Psalm 139:13–16**
     - ✓ We are the Creator's crowning act of creation on earth--the very best.
     - ✓ The thought that God took special interest to create us should boost our self-esteem. You should feel special no matter how you look. You are a child of God.

6. **How important is creation to the relationship between the Creator and us?**
   - **Isaiah 46:3–5**
     - ✓ The Creator invests time to walk with each one of us right through the journey of life from conception, birth, and even to our old age. He is in our lives full-time.
     - ✓ He promises to care for us and protect us from all the forces that threaten our lives.
     - ✓ There is no one who has our best interests at heart more than the Creator.
   - **Matthew 6:25–34**
     - ✓ Let's not allow worry to torment us as if we are all by ourselves in this world.
     - ✓ Even if all people desert you, God will still provide the care that you need. See also 1 Peter 5:7.
     - ✓ Trust that He who created you knows your needs better than yourself, and that He will provide them at His appointed time.
     - ✓ However, our relationship with Him should not major on material needs but on developing a rich spiritual relationship.
     - ✓ The Creator knows our future needs, so let's not suffer in advance because of our imagined or real future challenges. You do not know what a new day may bring to your life. Let go and let God. See also Psalm 46:1-3.

7. **Who deserves your worship?**
   - **Revelation 14:6–7**
     The Bible recommends that you should direct your worship to the Creator alone, because He is the one who created you. Your life is in His hands.

FOUND PEOPLE FIND PEOPLE

MEETING TWO

GOD'S REASON FOR CREATING US

1. **You need to understand God's personality in order to appreciate why He does things the way He does.**
   - **1 John 4:8**
     God is love. All His purposes and actions are motivated by love.

2. **How did God demonstrate His love towards us?**
   - **Romans 5:8**
   - **John 3:16**
     ✓ He does not love us because we are good or lovable. He loves you in spite of yourself.
     ✓ His love does not leave you the same. See Luke 19:1-10.

3. **What did God have in mind when He created humankind?**
   - **Genesis 1:26**
     ✓ He wanted us to be like Him. What a wonderful world this would be if we were all like God in thoughts, feelings, and actions.
     ✓ The act of creating us in His image shows the depth of His love for human beings.
     ✓ We were created to experience God's immeasurable love.

✓ The creation narrative is an expression of a loving Creator who is deeply in love with His creation.

4. **What qualities of God do we see in Jesus?**
   - Unconditional love – Romans 5:8
   - Forgiving – John 8:1-11
   - Selfless – Matthew 20:25-28
   - Humble – Philippians 2:5-8
   - Obedient – John 5:30
   - Sinless – Hebrews 4:15

5. **What does God intend to achieve through the life and character of Jesus?**
   - **1 John 2:6; Genesis 1:26**
     ✓ He wants to restore His image and likeness in us.
     ✓ Christ is God's character made visible. See also Matthew 1:23 and Colossians 1:15.

6. **What kind of life does God want us to enjoy?**
   - **Exodus 20:12–17**
     ✓ A life full of respect for one another.
     ✓ A life free from the fear of murder.
     ✓ A life free from adultery and sexual harassment.
     ✓ A life free from thieving and corruption.
     ✓ A life free from lying and falsehood.
     ✓ A life free from envy and jealous.

7. **How does the apostle Paul describe positive Christian life?**
   - **Romans 13:8–10**
     ✓ God wants us to have lives that reflect love for one another.
     ✓ There is no end to a life of love. See also 1 Corinthians 13:4-8.
     ✓ Love enables us to lead responsible lives.
     ✓ Love restrains us from causing unnecessary harm to our family members, relatives, friends, and neighbors.

8. **What is the main ingredient of love?**
   - **Deuteronomy 30:19**
     - ✓ Without the power of choice, there could be no true love.
     - ✓ God wants you to enjoy life and blessings.
     - ✓ While this is His choice for us, that certainly has to be your own choice too.
     - ✓ He will not force His way on you.
     - ✓ You are responsible for the consequences your choices bring into your life.
     - ✓ The best choice in life is to choose God.
     - ✓ When you have God, you have all the good that life has to offer.

9. **Since the Creator God is so passionate about loving us, what choice will you make today?**
   - **Joshua 24:15**
     Choose to fall in love with Him, even if the whole world were to forsake Him. He is your God and there is no other. See also Isaiah 46:9.

FOUND PEOPLE FIND PEOPLE

MEETING THREE

WHAT REALLY WENT WRONG?

The origin of pain and suffering on earth is the worst mystery in life. Many have tried to explain this mystery, but the Bible-believing Christians go by the account revealed by God in the Scriptures.

1. **Where was the first war fought in the universe?**
   - **Revelation 12:7–10**
     - ✓ The first war was fought in heaven itself.
     - ✓ It was between Christ and Satan.
     - ✓ It was not a physical war, because God cannot fight against His creation. No creature can match His power. He can just speak it out of existence without any resistance at all.
     - ✓ The war, mentioned in Revelation, must have been the struggle God went through to persuade a rebelling angel to live in harmony with the principles of heaven.
     - ✓ When all effort of love failed, God threw the Devil out of heaven because He could not co-exist with sin.

2. **Did God create the Devil?**
   - **Ezekiel 28:12–15**
     - ✓ No, He did not.
     - ✓ He created a perfect angel, full of beauty and wisdom.

- ✓ He was also perfect in character.
- ✓ This angel was God's best workmanship among all the angels.
- ✓ His name was Lucifer. See Isaiah 14:12.
- ✓ So God created Lucifer, not Satan.
- ✓ How Lucifer became Satan is a mystery.

3. **What hints does God give as some of the reasons for Lucifer's fall?**
   - **Ezekiel 28:17**
     Pride – he became self-centered or preoccupied with self because of his splendor.
   - **Isaiah 14:13–14**
     Envy – he wanted to be treated as God also.

4. **What is the core business of Satan?**
   - **Revelation 12:9**
   - **John 8:44**
     - ✓ He is a liar and the father of all falsehood.
     - ✓ He may even use truth to tell lies. See also 2 Corinthians 11:13-15.
     - ✓ He is doing everything to paint the Creator as a bad God who should not be trusted. See also Genesis 3:1-4.
     - ✓ Do not underestimate his deceptive power. He even managed to deceive some angels in heaven, who were then thrown out together with him. See Revelation 12:7-9.

5. **Does the Devil come to you in his true colors?**
   - **2 Corinthians 11:14**
     No, he comes disguised as a good guy.

6. **How did Satan approach Eve in the Garden of Eden?**
   - **Genesis 3:1–6**
     - ✓ He came in as a concerned fellow who had the best interests of Eve and Adam at heart.

- ✓ He presented God as someone who was out to cheat them.
- ✓ He convinced Eve that she needed true freedom and that freedom meant throwing away God's laws. According to the Devil's proposition, there seems to be a lot of fun outside God's restrictions.
- ✓ Eve fell prey to the Devil's deception, and she pushed her husband to do the same.

7. **What had God said to Adam and Eve before?**
   - **Genesis 2:15–17**
   Obey and live.

8. **Is it bad to give restrictions or laws to people?**
   - **Romans 13:10**
   Laws bring about social harmony. Without them, life can become chaotic and miserable.
   - **James 2:10–12**
     - ✓ Lawful restrictions safeguard real freedom. In other words, freedom without restrictions is chaos.
     - ✓ If you think that laws are bad, try to live in a lawless country.

9. **How is the Devil leading people into sin today?**
   - **Romans 1:18–32**
     - ✓ He wants us to dismiss the Creator out of our social lives and out of our religious lives.
     - ✓ His goal is to see people worshipping themselves or worshipping any other god, instead of the Creator.
   - **2 Timothy 3:1–5**
     - ✓ He wants people to live just for self and fun.
     - ✓ If we should worship the Creator, he does not want us to be totally committed to biblical values and principles. A religion of convenience is what he advocates, because he knows the Creator God does not approve of it.

- **Romans 1:18–32**
  The Devil has greater control over people who have less commitment to the Creator.

10. **What was the result of rebelling against God?**
    - **Genesis 3:17–19**
      Pain and death
    - **Galatians 5:19–21**
      Sinful nature
    - **Romans 3:23**
      Life that does not please God
    - **Romans 6:23a**
      Everlasting death. See also Revelation 20:14

11. **What is the fate of Satan and unbelievers?**
    - **Matthew 25:41; Revelation 20:9–10**
      They will be cast into the fires of hell.

12. **What should you do with Satan?**
    - **James 4:7**
      Resist the Devil in the name of Christ and he will flee.

MEETING FOUR

A FRIEND YOU CAN TRUST FOREVER

1. **Jesus is the complete opposite of Satan. He is a friend you need to trust for life.**
   What a friend we have in Jesus.

2. **Who is Jesus?**
   - John 1:1–3, 14
     - ✓ He is God.
     - ✓ He is the Creator. See also Colossians 1:15-16.
   - Matthew 28:19; 2 Corinthians 13:14
     - ✓ He is the Son of God and He is also part of the Godhead or the Holy Trinity.
   - Matthew 1:21; John 3:16.
     - ✓ He is the Savior of the world.
   - John 15:13–14
     - ✓ He is our Friend.

3. **Why do we need Jesus?**
   - Romans 7:15–25
     - ✓ He is the only solution to our sin problem.

4. **How does Jesus become a sin solution?**

- 2 Corinthians 5:18
  - ✓ God is reconciling the world back to Himself through Jesus.
- Romans 5:8; John 3:16
  - ✓ Jesus died in our place. We were supposed to have perished because of our sins. Thank God. We have the hope of everlasting life because of His death. See also Romans 6:23.
- Romans 8:3–4; Galatians 2:20; Romans 8:5–6
  - ✓ He is more than willing to enter into your life and help you experience victory over your carnal nature if you allow Him.
  - ✓ The Holy Spirit does this function on behalf of Christ.

5. **How can we tell that you are being transformed by Christ?**
   - **Galatians 5:22–23**
     You exhibit moral and spiritual transformation. Love, joy, peace, long-suffering, kindness, goodness, faithfulness, gentleness, and self-control become your second nature.
   - **Ezekiel 33:10–11**
     You make a U-turn in life, i.e. you turn from doing evil and start pursuing goodness.

6. **Is Jesus able to help the worst of sinners to change?**
   - **Luke 19:1–10**
     He changed Zacchaeus, one of the most corrupt business persons in biblical times.
   - **Luke 8:26–39**
     He delivered a man who was under the control of thousands of demons.
   - **John 4:1–42**
     He turned a sex worker into a mighty evangelist.
     He is able to change your life, too.

7. **How much does it cost to experience God's forgiveness and transforming love?**
   - **Ephesians 2:8–10**

It is free. Christ paid it all. You do not need to do anything to deserve God's favor. But His grace produces a good person out of you through the Holy Spirit.
- **1 John 1:8–9**
Confession of sins leads to reconciliation with God. Again, confession of any sin is free.

8. **What must you do to be saved?**
   - **Acts 16:29–31**
   The act of believing in Jesus alone is sufficient to be accepted back into God's family.
   - **Romans 10:13**
   You need to accept Jesus as your Lord and Savior.

9. **Please take a very important step and take Jesus as your friend today.**
Thank you for making this decision.

MEETING FIVE

AVOIDING RISKY BEHAVIORS

1. **Risky behaviors lead to serious consequences to self, others, and to the nation at large.**
   - A risky behavior is anything that leads to undesirable consequences.
   - Much of human suffering is avoidable.

2. **What are some of the risky behaviors discouraged in the Bible?**
   - **Proverbs 6:9–11**
     Laziness
   - **Proverbs 7:6–27**
     Sexual unfaithfulness
   - **Proverbs 23:29–35**
     Substance abuse
   - **1 Timothy 6:9–10**
     The love of money

3. **What solutions does the Bible offer to these challenges?**
   - **Proverbs 6:6–8**
     Lazy people need to learn from the ants. They are self-motivated and do not need someone looking over their shoulders in order to do their work.

- **1 Corinthians 7:2–5**
  Sex is restricted within a marital relationship comprising of one husband and one wife. The two of them are under obligation from God to fulfill their conjugal or sexual rights to each other. Sex should not be shared with any person outside the union of the two married parties. In the Bible, marriage is just between a male and a female – Genesis 1:2-28; Romans 1:18-28.
- **1 Corinthians 6:19–20**
  We need to treat our bodies with respect, out of reverence for God. You cannot do as you please with your body, because God says our bodies are His temple. The Holy Spirit dwells in us. See also 1 Corinthians 3:16-17; Romans 12:1-2.
- **1 Corinthians 10:31**
  Your drinking, eating, or whatever habits you may do should be within God's approval. Therefore, eat and drink to be in good health. Avoid habits that ultimately lead to lifestyle diseases. See also 3 John 2.
- **Ecclesiastes 2:1–11**
  Do not just live for money and pleasure. Have a much higher purpose in life. It's not money, but a God-directed purpose that gives meaning and fulfillment in life. If your whole reason for existence is just to be rich, then you are destined for vanity and emptiness, as King Solomon discovered. Some of the most miserable people on earth are also very rich. See also Ecclesiastes 5:10.
- **Deuteronomy 8:18; Ecclesiastes 5:19–20; Proverbs 20:21; Proverbs 13:11**
  Make God your wealth creation partner, and He will also give you peace.
- **1 Timothy 6:6–7**
  Learn to be content in life. The Bible is not saying have less. But you do not need to compromise your morals just for the sake of getting rich.
- **Proverbs 11:24–25**
  Generosity is the best way of receiving more. So wealth accumulation should not be an end in itself. God gives us more in order to bless others who are in need. See also Matthew 25:31-46.

4. **Where should you go in order to overcome bad habits?**
   - **Matthew 11:28–30**
     Jesus is the One you need to depend on in order to overcome the wrong habits that often depress or cause emptiness in your life. He is the real source and means by which you get real happiness and peace. A godly life is not burdensome, but it is the way to real satisfaction and joy even in the face of challenges. See also John 14:27 and Romans 5:1-5.

5. **Choose a habit that you want Jesus to help you overcome.**
   Thank you for taking a step that will make a big difference in your life. Many more victories will come your way as a result of the decision you have made today. God bless you.

FOUND PEOPLE FIND PEOPLE

MEETING SIX

YOUR SAFEST GUIDE TO LIFE AND REAL PEACE

1. We are now living in a world where it is continually getting harder to know what is right or wrong and what is true or false. Fortunately, the Bible is still around to guide us through life situations.

2. What object best symbolizes the Bible?
   - **Psalm 119:105**
     The Bible is viewed as the light that brightens the way along the path of life.

3. Who invented the **Bible?**
   - **2 Peter 1:19–21**
   - **2 Timothy 3:16**
     The Holy Spirit wrote the Bible through the prophets, the apostles, and many others.

4. In other words, the Bible is God's speech to us presented through human agents (writers) and language.
   - **Jeremiah 1:1–3**

- **Ezekiel 1:1–3**
- **Hosea 1:1**
  All these prophets introduce their books as "the word of the LORD."

5. **What is God's primary reason for producing the Bible?**
   - **John 17:3**
     The Bible reveals God.
   - **John 4:23**
     The Bible is the revelation of God's will and truth.
   - **John 17:17**
     The Bible is the tool in God's hands to lead us into a life of holy living.

6. **How does God view those who intentionally distort Scripture?**
   - **2 Peter 3:15–16**
     God is not happy when we twist the meaning of Scriptures to suit our biases.
   - **Revelation 22:18–19**
     Adding or subtracting what God intends the Scripture to inform us is met with His wrath.

7. **Is it safe to base our beliefs on human teachings?**
   - **Matthew 15:8–9**
     Human teachings that do not represent the truths embedded in the Bible should not be used to guide the Christian faith in matters of doctrine.
   - **Matthew 7:21–23**
     Religious leaders should not be trusted simply because they perform mighty miracles and wonders. The will of God is the ultimate test of all true worship.

8. **Why do we need the Bible?**
   - **2 Timothy 3:15–17**

- ✓ It makes us knowledgeable of salvation and doctrine.
- ✓ It rebukes us.
- ✓ It corrects us.
- ✓ It instructs us in matters of righteousness.
- ✓ It equips us for works of goodness.
- **Psalm 119:11**
  It keeps us from sinning against God.
- **2 Corinthians 1:20**
  It reveals God's promises.
- **Amos 3:7**
  It reveals the secret things of the future.
- **Revelation 1:1–3**
  It reveals Jesus Christ and the events that will lead to the end of the world.

9. **Do we still need the Old Testament?**
   - **2 Peter 1:19–21**
     The apostle Peter encouraged the New Testament believers to pay attention to the prophetic word of God. He said this at a time when the Old Testament books were the books most commonly used in churches. The New Testament was still being written. His counsel confirms the relevance of the Old Testament throughout the life of the church.
   - **John 5:39**
     The Old Testament is the foundation upon which the life and ministry of Jesus is built. We can only understand where we are going by understanding where we came from.
   - **Luke 4:17–21**
     Jesus used the Old Testament during His earthly life.
   - **Acts 2:14–21**
     - ✓ The Old Testament helps us understand the events in the New Testament better.
     - ✓ Both the Old and the New Testaments paint a bigger picture of God's revelation in human history. One testament by itself is not complete without the other.

10. **How powerful is the word of God?**
    - **Hebrews 4:12**
      The Bible is like a double-sided sword. It cuts right through us, into our hidden thoughts, and transforms them according to God's will. Since it was inspired by God Himself, it also has divine impact on the mind of the reader. It does not leave you the same when you read it prayerfully, with a mind that is ready to hear God speak.

11. **How often should we read the Bible?**
    - **Psalm 119:147–148**
      Read the Bible daily. Set special moments for study and meditation that suit your lifestyle. However, early morning and late at night tend to give quiet, undisturbed moments to be alone with God.
    - **Deuteronomy 6:6–7**
      Read the Bible daily as part of family worship. The Bible is a training guide for parenting. It contains values and principles that prepare children to live successfully in a hostile and corrupt world. There is no book that develops character better than the Bible.

12. **How important is it to share the word of God with others?**
    - **Romans 10:11, 13–15; Matthew 28:18–20**
      Anyone who meets Jesus through the revelation from the Scriptures is under obligation from God to go and share the same with others.

13. **Thank you for your wiliness to personally read the Bible and share it with others.**

MEETING SEVEN

ENJOYING GOOD HEALTH

1. Health is wealth and without good health the richest person is poor. Some anonymous person once said, "People who spend their health in search of wealth end up spending their wealth in search of health."

2. **What is God's wish for your health?**
   - 3 John 2
     God wishes that you may prosper in good health as you should in other areas of life.

3. **How best can you experience good health?**
   Try C.E.L.E.B.R.A.T.I.O.N.S. (Adapted from the Adventist Health Ministries) which stands for:
   - CHOICES
   - EXERCISE
   - LIQUIDS
   - ENVIRONMENT
   - BELIEFS
   - REST
   - ATTITUDE, ABSTINENCE AND AIR
   - TEMPERANCE AND TRUST IN DIVINE POWER

- **INTEGRITY**
- **O**PTIMISM
- **N**UTRITION
- SOCIAL SUPPORT SYSTEMS

4. **C.E.L.E.B.R.A.T.I.O.N.S. in detail:**
   - **Choices**
     Learn to make right choices in life – Micah 6:8; Deuteronomy 30:19.
   - **Exercise**
     ✓ Consult your doctor before embarking on a strenuous program.
     ✓ A daily session of 30 to 60 minutes of physical exercise is highly recommended.
     ✓ Brisk walking is one of the most beneficial and least expensive types of exercises.
   - **Liquids**
     Drink enough water to keep your urine clear.

5. **Environment**
   - Avoid all forms of pollution. Manage the environment well – Genesis 1:26–28.

6. **Beliefs**
   - Base your life on a belief system that promotes sustainable success across situations – Philippians 4:8.

7. **Rest**
   - Avoid overworking. Take time to rest since rest is meant to renew your energy and make you more productive – Exodus 20:9–10; Matthew 11:28–30; Isaiah 40:31.

8. **Attitude, Abstinence and Air**
   - **Attitude:** Avoid negative feelings towards self and others – Proverbs 14:30.

- **Abstinence:** Abstain from all risky behaviour.
- **Air:** 1. Air treat your rooms to kill germs. 2. Exercise cleans your lungs.

9. **Temperance and Trust in Divine Power**

   Temperance
   - Avoid going to extremes that negatively affect your health.
   - Exercise self-control in all things - Galatians 5:22-23.

   Trust in Divine Power
   Do your best to be in good health and leave the rest with God - Romans 12:1-2; James 5:13-16; 2 Corinthians 12:7-10.

10. **Integrity**
    - Know and do what is right even if the going is tough- Proverbs 11:3.
    -

11. **Optimism**
    - Generally expect things to go well for you despite the challenges that you may be facing from time to time - Romans 5:1-5; Romans 8:28, 37-39; 2 Corinthians 4:16-18.

12. **Nutrition**
    - Let your diet cover all the food groups.
    - Eat a variety of food from each food group.
    - Depend on plant-based foods as much as possible - Genesis 1:29.
    - Avoid taking flesh products from the animals that God regards as unclean:
      - ✓ Leviticus 11:1-30.
      - ✓ Deuteronomy 14:4-20.
      - ✓ Please note that God classified animals as clean and unclean before the Jewish nation came into existence. See Genesis 7:1-3.

- ✓ Mark 7:1-15; Acts 10:1-43 and Colossians 2:14-17 do not authorize Christians to eat anything that they can take to their mouths. If you read all the verses in each of the chapters provided above, you will notice that they are not dealing with issues of diet but are addressing other important matters.
- ✓ So the principle of dividing animals as clean and unclean has not been abolished.
- People who eat animal flesh should also take certain precautions:
  - ✓ Avoid eating anything that dies of itself – Deuteronomy 14:21. You may contract the terrible diseases that kill animals.
  - ✓ You are not allowed to eat blood – Genesis 9:3-4; Leviticus 17:12-14. Most impurities and disease causing organisms are concentrated in the blood.

13. **Social Support Systems**
    - Develop and maintain relationships that you can fall back on in times of need – Acts 2:44-46.

14. **Take a step to take care of your body in the manner that gives glory to God your maker.**
    - Read Romans 12:1-2.

15. **Thank you for making your health a priority.**

MEETING EIGHT

DOES THE SABBATH MATTER ANY MORE? PART 1

1. **Relevance of the Sabbath in today's world**
   The Sabbath is probably one of the most controversial topics among the Bible-believing faiths today. Some feel that it is a day of worship just for the Jews. Others think that it is a day of worship for all human beings, regardless of nationality. Others argue that every day is a day of worship, thereby nullifying the idea of a weekly Sabbath cycle. Some have come to believe that Jesus Himself is the Sabbath. So there is no point in observing a day which may be regarded as the Sabbath. There should certainly be a way of resolving this controversy.

2. **What is the practical way of solving this challenge?**
   - **Micah 6:8** - We need to be guided by God's revelation on matters of right or wrong.
   - **2 Timothy 3:15–17** - We need to be guided by the Bible on matters of doctrine.
   - **John 16:13** - We should seek the Holy Spirit to guide us in the search of truth.
   - **Matthew 15:9; Isaiah 8:20** - We should not trust any teaching or interpretation that is not supported by the Holy Scriptures.

- **1 Corinthians 10:11** - We need to learn from how the church throughout the Bible times (Genesis - Revelation) viewed the whole issue of the Sabbath.

3. **What caution should we exercise as we seek for biblical guidance on any matter?**
    - **2 Peter 3:15–16** - We should not twist the Scriptures to favor our own opinions or traditional views.
    - **Revelation 22:18–19** - We should not add or subtract to what God is saying in the Bible.

4. **What attitude should we have as we approach God's Word?**
    - We need to approach it with a learning spirit.
    - We need to read the Bible prayerfully.
    - We need to make a solemn declaration: "If the Bible says so, I believe it. If it is in the Bible, it is meant for me."

5. **What study method helps us study the Sabbath better?**
    - Let the Bible speak for itself.
    - Follow the historical path the Sabbath has taken from the very beginning.
    - Check for the reasons why the Sabbath was instituted in the Garden of Eden, and furthermore, check to see if the same reasons applied in both the Old and the New Testaments.

6. **What are the five major periods revealed in the Bible that have something to do with the Sabbath?**
    - The world before the fall of Adam and Eve into sin - **Genesis 2:1–3**.
    - The Old Testament time- **Ezekiel 20:12, 20; Isaiah 58:13–14**.
    - The New Testament Time- **Hebrews 4:9–11**.

- The period after Jesus' return to heaven – **Matthew 24:1–2, 15–22**.
- The world made new – **Isaiah 66:22–23**.

7. **What does the world before the fall of Adam and Eve teach about the Sabbath?**
   - **Genesis 1 – 2:1, 3; Exodus 20:8–11** - The Sabbath was the last day in the literal week of creation.
   - **Genesis 2:3; Exodus 20:11** - Of all the days of creation, God separated the Sabbath (seventh day) as a special and holy day unto Himself.
   - Both Genesis and Exodus see the Sabbath as God's act of celebrating creation.
   - So the Sabbath identifies the Owner of all the created works.
   - By keeping the seventh day holy, Adam and Even commemorated their creation and identified with their Creator.
   - **Genesis 2:15–17** - The Creator is the highest authority who deserves the right to give laws.
   - **Genesis 2:1–3** - The Sabbath was a literal 24-hour day and not a person.
   - **Genesis 2:1–3** - The Sabbath did not come into being because of sin or for the Jews. It was a universal day to be observed by humankind in a sinless world.

8. **What do we learn about the Sabbath from the Old Testament Time?**
   - **Exodus 31:13; Ezekiel 20:12, 20** -The Sabbath was a sign that separated the worshippers of the Creator from those that worshipped created things.
   - **Exodus 20:3–6** - The Old Testament considered the worship of anything other than the Creator as an abomination or an insult against God.
   - **Exodus 20:8–11** - The Sabbath was included by God in the Ten Commandments.

- **Exodus 20:11** - Of all the Ten Commandments, only the Sabbath identifies the Creator as the Law Giver.
- **Isaiah 46:3–9** - Creation is the foremost reason why one or something ought to be worshipped as God. This is the central message embedded in the Sabbath. See also Revelation 14:6-7.
- **Isaiah 58:13** - The Sabbath was a literal day of worship in the Old Testament. See also Leviticus 23:1-3.

9. **Was the Sabbath a special day in New Testament Times?**
   - **Luke 4:16** - Jesus traditionally observed the Sabbath as a special day of worship.
   - **Matthew 24:1–2, 15–20** - Jesus made it clear to His disciples that the Sabbath would still be in effect long after His return to heaven, as seen in His prediction of the destruction of Jerusalem in AD 70.
   - **Acts 17:2; 16:6–15** - Paul, the greatest evangelist of the New Testament times outside of Jesus, was a traditional Sabbath keeper and all the churches he planted in Asia and Europe were Sabbath-keeping churches.
   - **Acts 2:44–47; 13:14–16** - Although the saints could conduct prayer meetings daily, the Sabbath still remained as a special, regular day of worship.
   - **Mark 2:27–28** - Jesus never said He was the Sabbath, instead He said that He was the Lord of the Sabbath.
   - **Revelation 1:10** - John, the writer of the last book in the New Testament, recognized the Sabbath as the day of the Lord.
   - **Revelation 13:4, 6–8; 14:6–7** - The final conflict on earth will be a religious one focusing on the choice between worshipping the Creator on one hand and worshipping the Devil and his human agencies on the other. Hence, the need to keep the Sabbath as the reminder of the Creator-based worship.

- **Acts 16:13** - As with the Eden and the Old Testament churches, the New Testament was a Sabbath-keeping church. There was no departure from the norm. The Sabbath was a literal day and not Jesus Himself.

10. **Why is the period after the New Testament important to the Christian church with regards to the Sabbath?**

    This is the only period in the history of the Bible-based religion when attempts were made to replace the seventh day Sabbath with Sunday as a regular day of holy assembly.
    - ✓ Sunday has since become the special day of worship for many Bible-believing churches.
    - ✓ The Roman Catholic church is the only church on earth that officially claims to have solemnized Sunday as a special day of worship:
    - ✓ **The Convert's Catechism of Catholic Doctrine, 1957, p.57:**
        - ➢ Which is the Sabbath day?

          Saturday is the Sabbath day.

          Why do we observe Sunday instead of Saturday?

          We observe Sunday instead of Saturday because the Catholic Church transferred the solemnity from Saturday to Sunday.
        - ➢ **Catholic Record, September 1, 1923**

          Sunday is our mark of authority... The church is above the Bible, and this transference of the Saturday observance is proof of that fact.
        - ➢ **Decretal De Translate. Episcop. Cap**

          The Pope has power to change times, to abrogate laws, and to dispense with all things, even the precepts of Christ.
- **Did God foresee the change of the Sabbath coming into the world?**
    - ✓ **Daniel 7:25** -God revealed through Daniel the prophet, that attempts would be made to change the Ten Commandments.

- ✓ **2 Thessalonians 2:1–12** - Paul warned the Thessalonians that before the coming of the Lord, some religious powers will try to replace God in church affairs.
- ✓ **Daniel 7:25; Revelation 13:6** - No one is allowed to prescribe worship except for the Creator Himself, no wonder the Bible identifies anyone who attempts to do so as being blasphemous.
- ✓ If Sunday was supposed to be the regular special weekly day of worship, God was going to indicate it through the Bible prophets or apostles. He would not have left us to guess.
- ✓ Sunday worshippers are God's children, but Sunday itself is not the Lord's Day. Its solemnity as a day of worship above all other days of the week is a symbol of rebellion against the sovereignty of the Creator God.

11. **Will the Sabbath have any place in the earth and heaven made new?**
    - **Isaiah 66:22–23** - The Sabbath will be a regular day of worship for the redeemed eternally.
    - If Jesus was the Sabbath, there would be certainly no need for the Sabbath in the new heaven and the new earth.
    - In the restored universe, the Sabbath will still be regarded as a literal day of regular worship different from all the other weekly days.

12. **The Bible's position on the Sabbath is very clear**
    - The Sabbath started in the sinless world (Garden of Eden) and it will continue forever in the restored sinless universe (new earth and new heaven).
    - The Sabbath has been, and is, relevant to all human generations.

13. **What shall you do with the Sabbath?**
    - **Acts 17:30; Revelation 14:6–7; 18:4; John 10:16** – Accept it as the symbol of worship that esteems the Creator above

anything called god. The door of mercy is still open for God's children around the world to uphold true Bible-based worship. See also John 4:23.
- **Revelation 22:11** – Now that you know God's regular day of holy assembly, avoid taking chances. One day it will be too late to make the right decision. The door of mercy will close any time before the second coming of Christ and end of the world.

14. **Thank you for taking the bold step to worship God the Creator in spirit and in truth.**

MEETING NINE

DOES THE SABBATH MATTER ANY MORE? PART 2

1. **The challenges around the writings of Paul**
   A lot of people who experience some challenges of understanding the Sabbath are not to blame. The manner in which the apostle Paul presents his arguments in the New Testament confuses many of his readers including some theologians. This is why the apostle Peter (2 Peter 3:15-16) cautions us to read the writings of Paul with care, lest we make conclusions that are far from what Paul is teaching. The Sabbath and the law are some of the most problematic subjects in his letters. You need to really know the broader theme or issue he is dealing with in order to understand where he is coming from and where he is going with his arguments. This presentation is designed help you make the right conclusions on the Sabbath using the writings of Paul and of others.

2. **What is Paul's advice with regards to studying the Word of God?**
   2 Timothy 2:15 - You should do your best to handle the Scriptures correctly.

3. **Is there a way of handling the Scriptures so that you avoid distorting God's message?**
   Yes, there are several ways of doing that:

- Allow the Bible to interpret itself. If you do not understand what a writer is saying in some passage, you need to go to other passages where he explains the same topic in a clearer way. You can also follow the same theme across several Bible writers. You will see that comparing the books of the Bible along the same theme helps you to get a clear picture on issues. As an example, please read Daniel 7:1-3. What do the "beasts from the sea" mean? And what is the significance of the sea? Daniel 7:17 tell us that the beasts represent kings and Revelation 17:15 also says that large bodies of water represent nations in prophecy. So without comparing Scripture with Scripture, it would be very difficult to know what a writer is talking about.

- You also need to read the whole chapter or the whole book to understand the context under which the writer is saying whatever he is saying. It is not advisable to create a doctrine or teaching using just one text or chapter. Reading the whole chapter gives you the bigger picture the author is working on. Acts 10 is a classic example of this approach. If you just read verses 9-16 you may be tempted to think that God has permitted Christians to eat any animal that moves on the face of the earth. But when you read verses 24-29, you then notice that the vision of unclean animals is not specifically teaching Peter what animals to eat or not to eat. The vision was preparing him to start accepting non-Jews in Christian fellowship as opposed to the Jewish culture that viewed other races as religiously unclean.

- The other exciting method of understanding the Scriptures is a method I call the **The Law of Consistency**. The Law of Consistency picks a biblical idea or thought and follows it across the whole Bible to see if its meaning remains the same. Let's use the Ten Commandments as an example. Our interest is to check their permanency in Christian conduct and worship:

- ✓ **Exodus 20:1–17** - They were given by God Himself.
- ✓ **Exodus 20:3–17** - They are ten in number.
- ✓ **Exodus 34:28** - God wrote them on tablets of stone, suggesting permanency.
- ✓ **Jeremiah 31:31, 33** - The Ten Commandments are part of the new covenant.
- ✓ **Matthew 5:17–19** - Jesus said that He did not come to destroy the law or to remove anything from it for as long as the earth and heaven remain in existence.
- ✓ **Ephesians 2:8–10, Romans 3:31; 8:3–4** - Even though we are saved by grace through faith, Christians are still required to keep the commandments.
- ✓ **Romans 13:8–10** - The commandments are a manifestation of Christian character and love.
- ✓ **1 John 2:3–4** - The obedience, which is based on the commandments, confirms your knowledge of the Creator God.
- ✓ **1 John 5:3** - God still wants Christians to keep His commandments.
- ✓ **Revelation 14:6–7; James 2:10–12; Ecclesiastes 12:13–14** - Judgment will be based on our obedience to the commandments.
- ✓ **Revelation 14:12** - True worshippers accept Jesus by faith and express their obedience to God by keeping His commandments.

Please note that the permanency of the Ten Commandments throughout human existence is well established across the Bible. Therefore, Romans 6:14 does not mean that the commandments are done away with, but that our victory over sin is not based on our ability to obey God. We can't rely on our own righteousness to save ourselves--it is only on what Jesus Himself did and does on our behalf (see Galatians 2:20). Since the creation, the Sabbath remains part of the unchangeable commandments of God. Its permanency is also without question. The permanency of the

creation Sabbath has received great attention in the Bible:
- ✓ It was there in Eden.
- ✓ It was there in the Old Testament.
- ✓ It was there in the New Testament.
- ✓ It has always been kept after the New Testament times by those who understood its significance.
- ✓ It will be kept throughout eternity in the earth made new.

4. **So what does Paul mean in Colossians 2:16?**
   - At face value, this is what this text is saying:
     - ✓ When it comes to eating, Christians are free to eat anything that can get into their mouths. They are a rule unto themselves.
     - ✓ The day of worship is now left to individuals to decide since the Sabbath is done away with.

     These two assumptions do not represent what Paul means in this passage. So it pays to read the texts before and after verse 16.
   - Please read Colossians 2:14-17. What are the major thoughts from this passage that help you to understand the correct meaning of verse 16?
     - ✓ In verse 14, Paul is saying that the system of worship that was carried out in the form of ordinances or burdensome ceremonial requirements, which was stipulated for the Jews, became void when Christ died on the cross. Those ceremonies served no purpose after the cross.
     - ✓ In verse 15, Paul is elevating the death of Christ as the only means by which the demonic powers were overcome. Salvation is only through Christ the true Sacrificial Lamb from God (John 1:29). We are not saved by the blood of sheep and goats.
     - ✓ In verse 17, Paul says that the Jewish sacrificial system, which was based on burnt offerings of animals during certain times of the day, month, or season, only served to lead the Jews to understand the real Sacrificial Lamb in the person of Jesus Christ. So the symbols that represented Jesus became outdated since the real offering was sacrificed on the cross.

- ✓ In verse 16, Paul now groups all the ceremonies that accompanied Jewish religious system and declares them null and void because of the death of Christ. These ceremonies had eating and drinking requirements; some of the ceremonies were done during special festivals. The festival days were also known as *sabbath* days because people were not allowed to work during those festival days. In the Jewish culture, any day that would be set aside for rest to observe a religious ceremony would also be viewed as a day of rest or a *sabbath* day. No wonder in some translations the word *sabbath* in Colossians 2:16 NKJV is not capitalized. Even though the word *sabbath* is capitalized in Colossians 2:16 in the NIV, it is still put in a manner that separates it from the regular Sabbath of the LORD. The NIV puts it as *a Sabbath day* not the Sabbath day. Paul was not using *sabbath* days in reference to the creation Sabbath, but to ceremonial days or *sabbaths*.
- ✓ Leviticus 23:4-44 give a list of these feasts. Please pay attention to verses 26, 32, 37, and 39.
  - ➢ Do you notice that the ceremonial feasts are considered as holy days or *sabbath* days?
  - ➢ These *sabbath* days do not follow the weekly cycle as with the creation Sabbath of the Ten Commandments. They fall on any day of the week.
  - ➢ The Day of Atonement falls on the 10th day of the seventh month and that day is regarded as a *sabbath*.
  - ➢ The Feast of Tabernacles started on the 15th day of the seventh month and continued for eight days. So the 15th was the official opening day, and it too was regarded as a *sabbath*.
  - ➢ Do you see that the *sabbath* days of these two feasts are separated by just five days? But the creation Sabbath comes after every seven-day cycle.
  - ➢ Leviticus 23:38 clearly states that these festival *sabbaths* are outside the normal Sabbaths of the LORD.

- ✓ If you read the whole book of Acts, you will see clearly the bigger problem Paul was dealing with among the Jews. They did not want to let go of their ceremonial customs and days. They viewed these customs as more important than Jesus Himself.
- ✓ So, Paul had no problems with the creation Sabbath, which forms part of the Ten Commandments. He kept it himself and also planted Sabbath-keeping churches. But he was forthright in opposing the festival *sabbaths*.

5. **What day of the week does the creation Sabbath fall on?**
   - Exodus 20:8–11; Genesis 2:1–3 - The Bible says that the Sabbath falls on the seventh day of the week. This is the day of the week the Creator God chose from the beginning. Dictionaries show that Saturday is the seventh day of the week.
   - The calendars used to place Sunday as the first day of the week and Saturday as the seventh day of the week. That has since been changed as we now see Monday appearing as the first day of the week and Sunday as the seventh day of the week. This amendment will not change the fact that the Sabbath falls on Saturday no matter how people try to shift the order of days. Daniel 7:25 warn us that some powers will attempt to change God's times and laws.
   - The Easter holiday, whose days are ordered according to the death and resurrection of Jesus (John 19:31, 40-42 and Luke 24:1-7), shows that Saturday is the Sabbath day--since Jesus died on Friday and resurrected on Sunday, the first day of the week.

6. **Is it advisable to remain a member of a church that keeps a separate day of worship other than the Sabbath?**
   - Revelation 18:1-4
   - Matthew 7:21-23; 15:9.

- Amos 3:3
- John 4:23
- John 10:16
- Ephesians 4:3-6

What do you think God expects you to do? Do the right thing.

7. **Thank you for taking time to make a decision that will make a huge difference in your Christian journey.**

FOUND PEOPLE FIND PEOPLE

MEETING TEN

BECOMING A NEW PERSON

1. **The pain of being human**
    Many people, if not all, would hide if their private lives were to be made public by God. Others already lead public lives that are causing them pain because they feel guilty and ashamed of themselves. They have made several attempts to change themselves, but with little to no success at all. Some of the mental health challenges people face come from the perennial failure to become the kind of people who relate well with God, self, and others. The Bible is the book of hope. The worst of sinners can still become the best of saints if they allow God to turn their lives around.

2. **How does the Bible describe the number one human struggle?**
    - **Romans 7:15–24**
        - ✓ Some people we see struggling with bad habits actually do not like doing those things. They have simply lost the internal battle. Their willpower gets overcome by passions beyond their ability to control.
        - ✓ There is nothing wrong with the laws of God. The actual problem is that our sinful nature can't help us keep them, no matter how hard we try.

- ✓ Our bodies and minds are naturally inclined to sin. The truth of the matter is that sin unconsciously motivates our behavior to do wrong things.
- ✓ The most painful thing is that the knowledge of what is right and wrong, including our will to do what is right, still leaves us stuck in wrong behavior. Knowledge alone does not change human sinful nature.

- **Galatians 5:19–21**
  - ✓ If God does not help us, our nature has no choice but to continue doing evil until we die.
  - ✓ We risk losing everlasting life if we remain under the control of our evil nature.

3. **What process should you follow to experience freedom from the power of sin?**
   - You need to be born again:
   John 3:1–5
     - ✓ Please take note that Nicodemus was a spiritual leader, yet he was not born again.
     - ✓ We do not hear that he smoked or drank, but his life (thoughts, feelings or actions) was not pleasing before God.
     - ✓ A new self is a product of the Holy Spirit accompanied by water baptism.
     - ✓ A life that is under the control of the Holy Spirit does the things that are in line with the will of God. See also Romans 8:5.

   - You need the Holy Spirit to lead you to repentance:
     - ✓ **John 16:7–8** - The Holy Spirit is the one who convicts you of sin. He gets you to a point where you hate sin.
     - ✓ **Acts 2:36–37** - The Holy Spirit turns your conviction into a desire to seek forgiveness from God.
     - ✓ **Acts 2:38–39** - Your desire to seek forgiveness from God must be accompanied by the willingness to repent - i.e. to

start living a victorious life in Christ Jesus on a daily basis. The willingness to repent is also a gift from God. See also Philippians 2:13.
- ✓ **Acts 8:36–37** - Baptism is a public event which confirms your new relationship with God through Christ.

4. **What does baptism symbolize?**
   Romans 6:3–6; Colossians 2:13.
   Baptism symbolizes a funeral and a resurrection:
   - Your decision to leave a life of sin is a symbol of dying to your old self.
   - A dead person needs to be buried. So the act of being immersed under the baptismal water signifies the burial of your old self.
   - The act of being raised out of water represents the resurrection of your new self.
   - The whole act of baptism allows you to symbolically participate in the death, burial, and resurrection of our Lord Jesus Christ.

5. **Does baptism make you a perfect person the moment you get out of the water?**
   - **2 Peter 1:3–10; 3:18**
     - ✓ Perfection is a lifetime process.
     - ✓ Your life after baptism is expected to lead to the newness of life that grows daily in the grace and knowledge of Christ.
   - **1 John 1:8–9; 2:1–2** - You may still make some mistakes that offend God and others, even after baptism. Hence, the need for confession.
   - **1 Corinthians 10:13** - However, born-again Christians strive at all cost to avoid committing sinful acts willingly and knowingly. They need to pray for victory over all temptations.
   - **Galatians 5:22–23** - Those who are born of the Holy Spirit produce the character that pleases God.

6. **What are the conditions that must be met before you get baptized:**
   - **Acts 8:27–35** - You should have a doctrinal understating of Christ and salvation.
   - **Acts 8:36–37; 16:29–31** - You should believe in Christ.
   - **Acts 2:38** - You should repent.
   - **John 3:23; Matthew 3:16** - See that there is enough water to submerge you.
   - **Acts 2:47** - You should be willing to be part of the body of Christ, i.e., part of His church.
   - **Matthew 28:18–20** - You should be willing to serve God and humanity as a true disciple of Christ.

7. **What are the don'ts of baptism?**
   - Baptizing infants. They have no idea of sin.
   - Baptizing people who have not known Christ, including his fundamental truths.
   - Baptizing people using methods that do not completely immerse them underwater.
   - Baptizing people who feel no need for repentance.

8. **Does God allow people to be re-baptized?**
   - **Acts 19:1–5**
     You should be baptized again if your first baptism was not correctly done.
   - **Acts 2:37–38; 22:16**
     People who are joining a new faith may do so by being baptized again.

9. **Is it your pleasure to publicly confirm, through baptism, that Jesus is Lord and is it also your desire to worship God in truth as taught by the Bible? If it so, thank you for your willingness to renew your relationship with the Creator God. May He continue to bless you in your Christian journey.**

MEETING ELEVEN

THE PAIN OF LOSING LOVED ONES THROUGH DEATH

1. **The mystery called death**
   It is hard to get used to losing loved ones through death, no matter how many times you go through the experience. Some people go through unbearable grief with each loss. The other difficult part is that there are a lot of diverse teachings about death. Some of the teachings are quite frightening. Some people believe the dead are not quite dead, but alive in a different state. Some believe you can even speak to them if desired. Because the dead are alive, they can actually punish you for the wrongs you did to them while they were still living. Some misfortunes are attributed to angry spirits of the dead. Others speak of ghosts and mysterious human forms that appear to be the images of the dead. What would you do if you got to your bedroom at night and discovered that your relative, who died a long time ago, is sitting on the bed waiting for you?

   Some teach that the dead are really dead. Yet others still believe that there are no conscious spirits of dead people, but supernatural demonic spirits that act like our dead loved ones. Others believe that death is the end of everything. Some disagree with this view and feel that death is just a phase. Will God bring the dead back to life again?

2. **There are two common views on death:**
   - Spiritualism: The dead are alive in spirit form.
   - Biblical view: The dead are completely dead (unconscious state).

3. **Spiritualism says:**
   - The body dies, but the spirit remains alive.
   - The spirit of the dead operates as a conscious person.
   - The spirit goes about interacting with other spirits, including the people who are not yet dead.
   There are some evidences that some people attach to spiritualism:
   ✓ Ghosts and voices
   ✓ Visions and dreams
   ✓ Blessings and curses associated with the dead

   - What does spiritualism lead its believers to do?
     ✓ They consult the dead on some family or life issues.
     ✓ They seek to be protected by the dead.
     ✓ They appease the dead to avoid retribution.
     ✓ They worship the dead to receive blessings.

4. **What does the Bible say about the dead?**
   - **Ecclesiastes 9:5–6, 10** - The dead are really dead. They know nothing.
   - **Ecclesiastes 3:18–20** - The way animals and people die is the same.
   - **Job 7:9–10; 14:10–12** - The dead do not awake from their graves.

5. **How does the Bible help us to understand what happens at death?**
   To understand what happens at death, you should know the formula God used to create human beings - Genesis 2:7 New King James Version:

- ✓ God used dust (chemicals and minerals) to form the human body.
- ✓ He breathed into Adam life (life is the life giving energy or power that only comes from God the source of life). Other versions say the spirit of life. The word breath and spirit are interchangeable. Both refer to life in Genesis 2:7.
- ✓ Please note that the Bible does not say that God breathed into man a living spirit. He breathed life.
- ✓ Dust + Life = A living person.
- ✓ So at death, the reverse order happens - Ecclesiastes 12:7
  - ➢ Dust goes back to the ground where it came from.
  - ➢ Life goes back to God the source of life.

6. **Does the death of Christ help us to understand what happens to the dead?**
   - His death happened exactly like the explanation you find in Ecclesiastes 12:7.
     - ✓ **Luke 23:46** - His life returned to God the source of life. It did not go there as Jesus in spirit form. It was just life. Do not be confused when He says "spirit" instead spirit of life. The word spirit means a lot of things. So the context of the passage decides its meaning. Follow this discussion closely, and you will notice that spirit here just refers to life and not a living person in spirit form.
     - ✓ **Luke 23:52–53** - His body was buried in a grave.
   - One of the problems around the death of Jesus was the statement He made to one of the criminals who was also dying on the cross next to Him - Luke 23:42-43
     - ✓ The statement seems to confirm that people go to heaven immediately after death. It appears that Jesus and the criminal in question were just waiting for their bodies to die in order to fly to heaven as spirits. This is far from the truth. None of them were going to heaven that day after death. When the original Bible writers were writing, they did not use punctuation

marks (like the comma) as we do today. The commas were inserted recently by the translators. The comma in verse 43 is misplaced. Instead of "Assuredly, I say to you, today you will be with Me in paradise." It should be, "Assuredly, I say to you today, you will be with Me in paradise." The position of the comma changes the whole meaning.
- **Read John 20:1–7, 11–17 carefully.**
  - ✓ Do you notice that the body of Jesus is no longer in the tomb because He has been resurrected?
  - ✓ He did not just disappear into heaven. He waits for His disciples to witness that He is alive again.
  - ✓ The same body that had died is the same one that awakes.
  - ✓ He tells Mary Magdalene that He has not yet gone to heaven ever since His death and His resurrection.
  - ✓ He sends Mary to announce His trip to heaven to the other disciples after resurrection.
  - ✓ So the spirit that He committed into His Father's hands when He died on a Friday had no personal identity at all. It was just formless life that would neither speak nor remember anything.
  - ✓ Thank God, the death of Jesus has left lessons that should guide us in understating death.
  - ✓ One of the biggest lessons is that outside of resurrection by the act of God, the dead remain in the state of complete silence and unconsciousness. And nobody goes to heaven and leaves their bodies behind - 1 Corinthians 15:51-55.

7. **If the dead are really dead, how does the Bible explain the mysteries that surround death like voices, ghosts, and the like?**
   - **Revelation 12:7–12**
     - ✓ The whole universe is in a great controversy between Christ, the Prince of Light and Satan, the prince of darkness.
     - ✓ The Devil and his demons are great architects of deception.

- ✓ They use death as a platform to mislead multitudes away from the Creator God and from true worship.
- **1 Samuel 28:3–20**
  - ✓ This narrative unveils what happens in the underworld where the powers of darkness are in control.
  - ✓ Imagine, God is not willing to communicate with Saul using any form of communication, including His priests and prophets, but a spirit medium is able to raise Samuel from among the dead to speak with Saul.
  - ✓ How can Samuel be found working in partnership with the enemies of God?
  - ✓ When Samuel wakes up, he tells Saul exactly what is going to happen the next day.
  - ✓ The Devil is so subtle and cunning. He can use truth to deceive many.
  - ✓ The old man who appears on the wall is not Samuel, but a counterfeit spirit.
  - ✓ One of the demons posed as Samuel.

8. **What is the Bible's advice on consulting spirit mediums or the dead?**
   - **Deuteronomy 18:9–12; Isaiah 8:19**
   Do not play with fire. Avoid dabbling in mediums or spirits at all cost. Anyone who goes or remains there becomes an enemy of God and no enemy of God will have peace in this world, no matter what benefits the Devil gives. His benefits always turn out to be curses in the end.

9. **Is it safe to return to God after one has joined the wrong camp?**
   - **Luke 8:26–39; Revelation 12: 7–10** - Christ is more powerful than Satan.
   - **Mark 16:15–18; Revelation 12:11** - Christ gave His church power over the forces of darkness.

10. **Is death the end of everything?**
    1 Thessalonians 4:13–18
    Christians have the hope that someday soon the world will end, and God will resurrect our dead loved ones back to life. What a great reunion it will be as we shall live forever together with Christ our Savior. See also Revelation 21:1-5.

11. **Please make every effort to make the hope in 1 Thessalonians 4:13–18 your personal hope by choosing to confess Jesus as your Lord. Thank you for taking this giant step in your life.**

MEETING TWELVE

UNDERSTANDING OUR TIMES

1. **A planet in crisis**
   There is so much happening in our world that baffles the minds of many people. Think of the wars in the Middle East--the political world is in turmoil indeed. When it comes to social life, we see immorality surging at an alarming rate. People are now free to be anything, or to do anything, in the name of democracy and human rights. Marital failure has never been this bad. Distress and depression seems to be the order of the day in many families. On a different note, natural disasters are rampant. They are leaving cities in ruins and millions homeless. Diseases are also taking their toll in terms of millions of deaths per year. What exactly is happening? What does the future hold for us?

2. **Does the Creator know what the future holds?**
   - **Isaiah 46:9–10** - God knows the future before it comes. Nothing is hidden from Him.
   - **Amos 3:7** - God does not want the future to come to us as a surprise. He reveals it in advance.

3. **Does the Bible have any clue as to why our world seems to be falling apart?**

- Jesus made some predictions about some of the things that the world has and is experiencing today:
  - ✓ **Matthew 24:4–5, 24** - Religion will be infiltrated by the representatives of Satan, who will lead millions to believe lies. Their deceptive efforts are accompanied by great miracles, signs, and wonders. Watch out if your religious interests are only centered on experiencing miracles instead of God's truth (see John 4:23-24; Matthew 7:21-23). You could be treading on a dangerous ground.
  - ✓ **Matthew 24:6–7a** - The world will be a boiling pot of political conflicts and wars.
  - ✓ **Matthew 24:7b**- Natural disasters will be widespread.
  - ✓ **Matthew 24:12** - Lawlessness and secularism will abound.
  - ✓ **Matthew 24:8** - World conditions will continue to worsen. There will be no permanent human solution to what lies ahead. We need to brace ourselves for tough times. Even the most powerful nations on earth will be shaken.
- The apostle Paul also made serious predictions about the future:
  - ✓ **2 Timothy 3:1–5**
    - ➤ Life on earth will become perilous as we near the end of the world.
    - ➤ People will become self-centered.
    - ➤ People will do anything to be rich. They will just live for money.
    - ➤ People will be irreconcilable because of pride.
    - ➤ People will lack self-control. They will behave in unthinkable ways.
    - ➤ People will not esteem human life. Murder will become a way of life.
    - ➤ People will have no interest in good social values and principles. Everyone will be a law unto himself.
    - ➤ People will prioritize pleasurable living above serving God.

- People will opt more for the religious life that will not disturb their worldly passions than for the one that fully surrenders to God's will. They will attend church, but spirituality, character, and truth will not be the main agenda.
- ✓ **2 Thessalonians 2:1–12**
  - Paul also points out that the church of God will be infiltrated by some disguised powers, which will only come in to further the cause of Satan.
  - The Devil himself will be the power behind the actions of these systems.
  - Their main strategy is to use signs and wonders just as Jesus warned before.
  - Miracle-hungry people will be an easy prey to deception.

- John, the writer of the book of Revelation, also made similar religious predictions as Jesus and Paul:
Please note that the book of Revelation thrives on prophetic symbols and imagery that require special attention. Actually, both Revelation and Daniel require separate studies. This presentation is too short to make you understand the essence of their prophetic messages. The reason for referring to the book of Revelation now is just to confirm that the Devil is real, and that he is going to push hard to be worshipped in the last days before Christ comes.
  - ✓ **Revelation 13:4, 7–8 (dragon: see Revelation 12:7–10; beast: see Daniel 7:15–17)**
    - The Devil will come up with a global religious system that will direct worship to him in disguise.
    - People who are not serious with their allegiance to God will be defenseless against the force to worship Satan, no matter what religion or denomination you may be coming from.
    - The drive to worship the Devil will be global, public, and enforced through unprecedented persecution.

- ✓ **Revelation 13:13–14**
  - ➤ Again, miracles are going to be used to lure people into false worship.
  - ➤ So miracles by themselves are not a sign of true worship - Matthew 7:21-23. The Devil also uses them to advance his cause - Matthew 24:24.

4. **What are all these global conditions mentioned by Jesus, Paul, and John, including others that we did not quote pointing to?**
   - **Matthew 24:3; John 14:1–3** - They all point to the coming of Jesus Christ to end this world.
   - **2 Peter 3:1–13** - Even if it appears that Christ has delayed His second coming, He is still coming.

5. **What global phenomenon will decide the end of the world?**
   - **Matthew 24:14; 28:18–20; Revelation 14:6–7** - The act of taking the gospel to all humankind within and across borders is more important to God in deciding the end of the world than all the other world conditions put together.
   - **2 Peter 3:9** - The salvation of every human being matters so much to God.

6. **Do we know exactly when Christ is coming?**
   - **Matthew 24:36** - Nobody knows except God.
   - **Matthew 24:37–39; 2 Thessalonians 5:1–4** - The day of Christ will come as a thief in the night to those who do not care or think about the end of the world.

7. **Since we do not know when Jesus is coming, what should we be doing in the meantime?**
   - **Matthew 24:44** - Be always ready for His coming.
   - **2 Peter 3:11–14** - Strive for holiness and godliness.

8. Matthew 10:34–39 - The issue of salvation is an individual matter. Please take a moment to ask Jesus to help you to prepare for His coming. His coming is real and you need to be real in your preparation. Thank you for making a bold decision to follow Jesus. It's not easy, but it's worth it.

FOUND PEOPLE FIND PEOPLE

MEETING THIRTEEN

THE PROMISE OF THE HOLY SPIRIT

1. **What was the greatest need of the church after the death of Christ on the cross?**
   - John 16:7–8, 12–13
     - ✓ The Holy Spirit convicts us of sin.
     - ✓ He convicts us of righteousness.
     - ✓ He convicts us of judgment.
     - ✓ He guides us to discover God's truth.
   - **Acts 1:8** - The Holy Spirit gives power to the church to carry out its mission.
   - **Galatians 5:22–23** - The Holy Spirit is the one who develops Christ-like character in all born-again believers.
   - **1 Corinthians 12:4–7, 11** - The Holy Spirit gives us spiritual gifts in order for each believer to serve God through various ministries.

2. **The focus of this presentation is on spiritual gifts:**
   - A spiritual gift is an ability which you can only receive by the act of the Holy Spirit for Christian service - 1 Corinthians 12:4, 11. It is not a natural talent that you receive from the genes of your parents.

- Spiritual gifts include, but are limited to the following:

1 Corinthians 12:8–10, 28– 30		Ephesians 4:11
Wisdom	Discernment	Apostles
Knowledge/Teaching	Tongues	Prophets
Faith	Interpretation of tongues	Evangelists
Healing	Apostleship	Pastors
Miracles	Administration	Teachers
Prophecy	Helping	

- Spiritual gifts function as the parts of the body:
    - ✓ **1 Corinthians 12:14–18** - Each believer is specifically gifted. One serves as an eye, another as a nose, and someone as a leg. No one should be idle.
    - ✓ **1 Corinthians 12:28–30; Ephesians 4:11–12** - Each believer is not meant to be all things to all people. There should be separation of duty for the edification of the church.
    - ✓ **1 Corinthians 12:7** - Gifts are meant to serve God and others. See also 1 Peter 4:10.

3. **Which is the greatest and only gift that should be in each believer?**
    - 1 Corinthians 12:31 – 13:1-13
        - ✓ While the gifts listed in 1 Corinthians 12 are important for the functioning of the church, there is a gift that far outweighs them all.
        - ✓ Love is the greatest gift.
        - ✓ It is utterly useless before God to have the gifts of prophecy, knowledge, tongues, or any other gift without love.
        - ✓ Love is the sign of true discipleship - John 13:35.

4. **What special recommendation does Paul give in 1 Corinthians 14:1?**

- Pursue love.
- Desire spiritual gifts.
- Pay special attention to the gift of prophecy.

5. **Why does he pull out the gift of prophecy specifically?**
    - **1 Corinthians 14:2, 4** - The gift of tongues had created some challenges in the Corinthian church, because those who were able to express themselves in foreign tongues were not using them to benefit fellow believers. They used this gift for personal edification.
    - **1 Corinthians 14:3** - The gift of prophecy benefitted the corporate body of believers. It provided edification, exhortation, and comfort to all the believers.
    - **1 Corinthians 14:5** - Paul had greater preference for the gifts that edify believers than those that do not serve a purpose for the common good of the church.

6. **What is the gift of prophecy?**
    - **John 5:39** - The gift of prophesy is the revelation of Jesus Christ, which is passed on to the church by the prophets. For example, the whole book of Revelation is a revelation of Jesus given through John - Revelation 1:1-2; 22:18-19.
    - The book of Revelation edifies the church - Revelation 1:3. So does any book of the Bible.
    - **Revelation 19:10** - The testimony or the teaching of the prophetic revelation of Christ is the heart of the gift of prophecy. Therefore, the gift of prophecy is not only about predicting the future. It also includes the ability to understand and to unpack the prophetic messages in the Bible that God intends for our edification.

    For instance, we need the gift of prophecy to really understand the books of Daniel and Revelation, which many Christian churches avoid at all cost. If any person claims to be a prophet, he should also be able to help us understand the messages of the other prophets in the Bible. See Revelation 1:1-3.

- So the teaching of believers to understand God's revelation is the very essence of prophecy.

7. **What should be done to make the gift of tongues relevant to the church?**
   - **1 Corinthians 12:7; Ephesians 4: 11–12**
     - ✓ Uphold the very reason why God gives gifts to the church.
     - ✓ Each gift is meant for ministry to the church.
   - **1 Corinthians 14:23** - The gift of tongues should not be done in a manner that causes the church to lose public respect.
   - **1 Corinthians 14:27** - The number of people who should speak in tongues, at any given time, should be limited to allow the church to benefit from each speaker.
   - What should happen if there is no one available to interpret tongues?
   - **1 Corinthians 14:28**
     - ✓ The person with tongues should remain silent in church.
     - ✓ But he is allowed to speak in tongues when he is alone.
   - **1 Corinthians 14:33** - Order is critical to any worship experience.

8. **What is the typical difference between the tongues in Acts 2 (at Pentecost) and those in 1 Corinthians 14 (at the Church of Corinth)?**
   - **Acts 2:1–12 - Pentecost:**
     - ✓ The gift of tongues was expressed in human languages.
     - ✓ The different nationalities did not need interpreters.
     - ✓ One speaker would speak and be heard by about seventeen different nationalities in their own mother languages.
   - The type of tongues in Acts 2 was a fulfillment of the promise made by Jesus to His disciples in Mark 16:15-18.
     - ✓ Jesus commissioned His disciples to take the gospel beyond the borders of Palestine.

- ✓ They were going to face language barriers as they went out with the gospel, hence the need of the gift to be heard by people of different languages.
  - ✓ So Jesus promised them the gift of other human languages.
  - ✓ This gift was confirmed at Pentecost in front of an audience that was coming from about 17 different nationalities, and three thousand of them were baptized after Peter's sermon - Acts 2:7-11, 38-41.
- **1 Corinthians 14 – The Corinthian Church**
  - ✓ Tongues were a departure from the norm, no wonder Paul took time to correct the situation.
  - ✓ The purpose of the gift moved from service to others and simply focused on personal edification.
- Given a choice between Corinthians and Acts, Paul would opt for the type of tongues in Acts because they benefitted the church (1 Corinthians 14:6-13). Besides, the gift of tongues is meant to help the church take the gospel to all language groups around the word - Matthew 28:19; Mark 16:15; Acts 1:8; Revelation 14:6.

9. **How can you discover your spiritual gifts (Adapted from the International Institute of Christian Ministries [IICM Module CR 101]?**
   - First of all, list all the spiritual gifts that can be found in the Bible, including any others that God can give to equip His church for service.
   - Take a spiritual gift test if you can find one. This is a questionnaire that you fill in and it gives scores that indicate the areas of your giftedness.
   - Be willing to try some activities you haven't done before. You may be surprised to discover that you possess a wonderful gift.
   - Check for the activities that you are passionate about. When God gives you a gift, He also makes you feel good about it,

even if there may be trying times. You should not be easily discouraged.
- Listen to the feedback you get from the church and from the other believers. If you are gifted in something, they will tell you in various ways.
- Pay attention also to the results that come after you do certain activities. A gifted person tends to generally get good results in the area of their giftedness.
- Last, but not the least, pray that God shows you your gifts.

10. **May you please aim for the highest gift—to love God and others unconditionally.**
See 1 Corinthians 13; Luke 10:27; 1 John 4:7-8. Thank you for your willingness to worship and to serve through love.

MEETING FOURTEEN

FREE AT LAST

1. **The hope that keeps us going**
   The apostle Paul is one of the most passionate writers in the Bible, who strongly believes that the hardships we face daily in life are just but a passing phase. The future holds greater joy beyond our wildest imagination. One day soon, we will shout free at last as heaven becomes real.

2. **How does the Bible describe our current experiences on earth?**
   - **Romans 8:22–23.**
     - ✓ The whole creation is subjected to suffering and pain.
     - ✓ Christians are also not spared from suffering.
     - ✓ This is the only planet that has known misery.
   - **Romans 5:12**
     Sin is responsible for all forms of suffering, including death.

3. **Is there hope beyond our suffering?**
   - **Romans 8:18**
     Today's suffering does not compare with the joy that we will experience when this world is made new.

- **2 Corinthians 4:16–18**
  - ✓ The hope of the new world gives us strength to accept our daily challenges.
  - ✓ God is faithful. He always turns our misfortunes to work in our favor. See also Romans 5:3-5; 8:28.
- **Titus 2:13**
  - ✓ The second coming of Christ is our most valued blessed hope.
  - ✓ This hope helps us to say no to the evil pleasures of this world.
- **1 John 3: 1–3**
  - ✓ Despite our suffering, God loves us.
  - ✓ We are His dear children.
  - ✓ One day, He will come to take us and we shall forever be with Him.
  - ✓ This hope purifies us.
- **John 14:1–3**
  - ✓ Jesus went ahead of us to prepare heaven as our dwelling place.
  - ✓ He promised to come back and take us home. See also Numbers 23:19.

4. **Will the coming of Christ be a private, secretive event?**
   - **Matthew 24:30–31.**
     - ✓ His coming is a global, visible event. Everyone will witness it. See also Revelation 1:7.
     - ✓ It will be a glorious event.
     - ✓ Angels will fill the sky like clouds at Christ's coming.
     - ✓ It will be a noisy event. See also 1 Thessalonians 4:16.
     - ✓ The redeemed will be gathered from all the directions of the earth.
   - **Matthew 24:25–27**
     - ✓ We are warned against believing that Christ's coming is going to be private.
     - ✓ The Devil will try to mimic the second coming of Christ through fictitious, private appearances in isolated parts of the world.

- ✓ Jesus Himself says that we should not even dare to believe such lies.
- ✓ His coming is characteristically global, visible, and audible.

5. **Who is Jesus coming for when He appears in the sky?**
   - **1 Thessalonians 4:15–18.**
     - ✓ He is coming to resurrect those who died believing in Him, whose names are in the Book of Life.
     - ✓ He will also take the righteous who are living, who will not yet have tasted death.
     - ✓ This means there will be a group that remains behind as the redeemed fly to heaven.

6. **Who will miss the flight to paradise?**
   - **Revelation 6:13–17**
     - ✓ While the redeemed rejoice at the coming of the Lord, all the people who took the gospel as a joke will not stand the reality of Christ's coming. They will be forever lost, and they will run away into hiding places. It will be a sorry sight to behold.
   - **Revelation 20:5**
     - ✓ The dead who were wicked will not resurrect with the redeemed at Christ's second coming.
     - ✓ They will remain in their graves for a thousand years.

7. **How does the Bible explain the two resurrections that will separate the righteous from the wicked?**
   - **Revelation 20:5–6.**
     - ✓ The resurrection of the redeemed is called the first resurrection.
     - ✓ Everyone who takes part in it is blessed because their resurrection leads to eternal life.
   - **Revelation 20:13–14.**
     - ✓ The second resurrection belongs to the wicked.
     - ✓ They will come back to life to face their punishment, which

is the second or eternal death through the consuming fire of hell.

8. **Who else will perish through hell fire?**
   - **Revelation 20:7–10**
     - ✓ Satan will also perish in hell.
     - ✓ Religious leaders who are responsible for leading people astray will also perish in hell.
   - **Matthew 25:41**
     - ✓ God has prepared hell just for the Devil and his demons.
     - ✓ Anyone who rejects the love of God will suffer the same fate.

9. **Will hellfire burn forever and ever?**
   - **Revelation 20:10, 14.**
     - ✓ The Bible would not be talking of the second death if hellfire would burn eternally.
     - ✓ The effect of hell-fire is the one that is forever. The existence of Satan and the wicked will cease eternally.
   - **Malachi 4:1–3**
     - ✓ Malachi says that the wicked will be destroyed until only ashes remain.
     - ✓ Hell will stop when its job is done and the redeemed will be able to go and inspect the damage caused by its fire.
   - **Ezekiel 18:23**
     - ✓ God does not enjoy seeing the people and the angels He once created perishing in hellfire. It will not be a day of rejoicing for Him. But it must be done.
     - ✓ This is why God is making every effort to win our hearts back to Him. See also 2 Peter 3:9.
   - **1 John 4:8.**
   God is love. Whatever He does is consistent with His nature.
   - **Revelation 21:1–2.**
   The creation of the new earth is also evidence that the old earth will not continue to burn forever.

10. **What good news does the new earth bring us?**
    - **Revelation 21:1–5.**
        - ✓ The end of human civilization, which is characterized with selfishness and misery is good news.
        - ✓ The thought that sin and the Devil will never exist again causes tears of joy.
        - ✓ Living and seeing God face to face is the dream of every believer. Nothing beats this expectation.
        - ✓ The extinction of death, pain, and mourning makes the second coming of Christ worth waiting for.
        - ✓ The thought of living forever is beyond human conception, and to be a part of that life brings eternal bliss.

11. **What does it take to be in heaven?**
    - **Romans 6:23; Ephesians 2:8–10**
        - ✓ Eternal life is a gift
        - ✓ It comes at Christ's cost. See also John 3:16; Romans 5:8.
        - ✓ You do not need to please God by some good acts in order to be in heaven.
        - ✓ All you need is to accept Jesus as your personal Savior. See also Acts 16:30-31.
        - ✓ However, the saved are loyal disciples who find joy in obeying their Master. See also John 14:15; Revelation 14:12.

12. **The choice is yours**
    - **Joshua 24:15**
        - ✓ God will not force you to go to heaven.
        - ✓ Heaven has to be your free, conscious choice.
        - ✓ Please make a choice today to spend eternity with Jesus and the redeemed.

13. **Thank you for your desire to experience JOY without an end! Meet you there.**

ABOUT THE AUTHOR

PASTOR MACKENZIE KAMBIZI BIO
Senior Pastor, Ethan Temple, Allegheny West Conference
Founder and Speaker Director of Truth for These Times Broadcast

PASTOR MACKENZIE KAMBIZI is a man of God whose life and ministry mission is to empower people to have a LIVING THRIVING RELATIONSHIP with God by increasing faith, instilling holiness, and inspiring hope. His personal philosophy is: "Bad news won't change my mind." He is a visionary shepherd, agent of compassion, theological ethicist, biblical expositor, revivalist, evangelist, conference speaker, congregational transformer, community developer, cultural critic, folklorist, and dramatist. He works from a practical, relevant, and biblical approach. Pastor Kambizi dares things most people do not see and dreams worlds that are beyond most people can imagine. He provokes thought through bold preaching, creative teaching, resourceful training, in-depth mentoring, and practical motivation. As a driven and guided leader with great passion and vast pastoral experience (internationally and locally), he attempts to do the extraordinary for God in his lifetime through faithful stewardship of influence, opportunity and responsibility. He strongly believes that the Church is the only organization that exists for its nonmembers and the community--our mission field. As a global evangelist, Pastor Kambizi is a strong proponent of evangelism and leadership development who has seen thousands of souls added to the church, and counts it an honor and a privilege to serve Jesus Christ in order to equip people for service.

BOOKS PUBLISHED:
Bad News Won't Change My Mind

<u>Books Coming Soon:</u>
Radical Release: Total Freedom through Total Forgiveness
The Lion Chaser
Waiting Without Worrying
Swimming with an Anchor – The Christian's Attitude Towards Suffering